ABC
BUG BOOK
FOR KIDS

Jessica Lee Anderson

R
ROCKRIDGE
PRESS

For general information on our other products and services or to obtain technical support, please contact our Customer Care Department within the United States at (866) 744-2665, or outside the United States at (510) 253-0500.

Rockridge Press publishes its books in a variety of electronic and print formats. Some content that appears in print may not be available in electronic books, and vice versa.

TRADEMARKS: Rockridge Press and the Rockridge Press logo are trademarks or registered trademarks of Callisto Media Inc. and/or its affiliates, in the United States and other countries, and may not be used without written permission. All other trademarks are the property of their respective owners. Rockridge Press is not associated with any product or vendor mentioned in this book.

Interior and Cover Designer: Linda Kocur
Art Producer: Maya Melenchuk
Editor: Laura Bryn Sisson
Production Editor: Ruth Sakata Corley
Production Manager: Jose Olivera

Please see page 56 for photo credits.

Paperback ISBN: 978-1-63878-066-3
eBook ISBN: 978-1-63807-671-1
R0

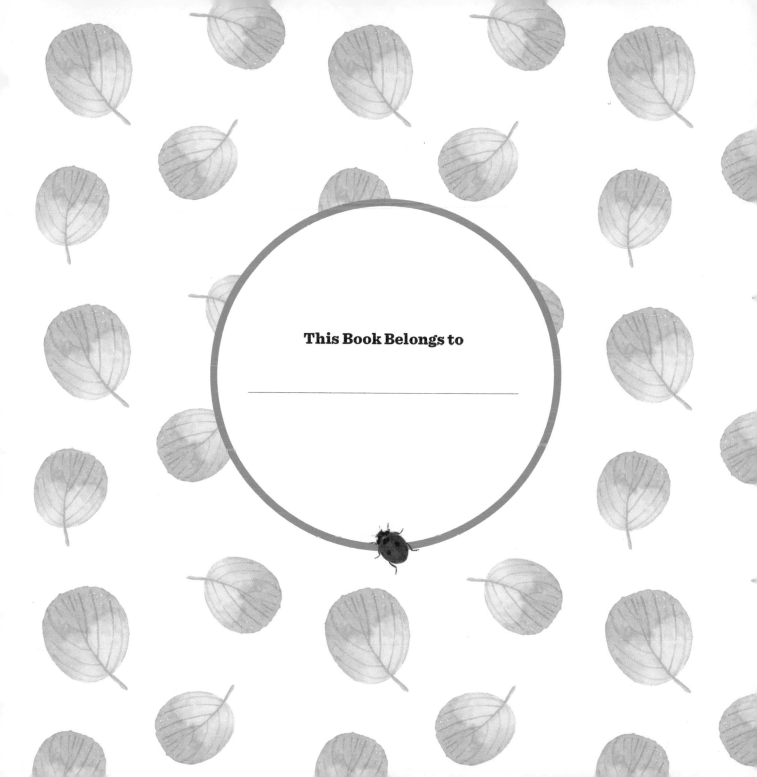

This Book Belongs to

_____

A is for **Ant**

Ants live in groups called colonies. They have jobs and work as a team.

Fire Ant

Honeypot Ant

B is for **Butterfly**

Eighty-Eight Butterfly

Butterflies find the perfect plant by tasting it with their feet as they land.

Blue Morpho Butterfly

C is for **Caterpillar**

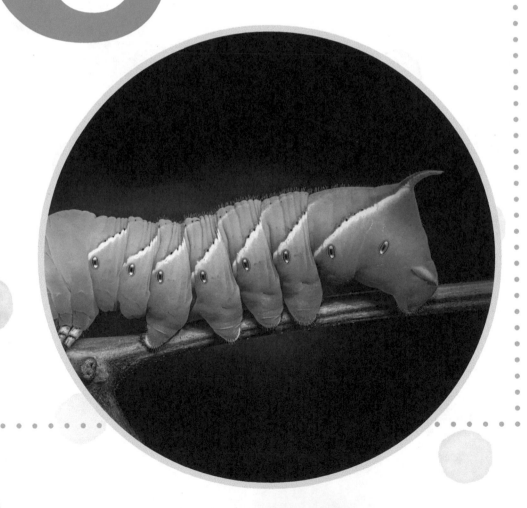

Yellow Coster Caterpillar

Caterpillars grow up to become moths or butterflies. They eat a lot!

Woolly Bear Caterpillar

D

is for Dragonfly

Widow Skimmer Dragonfly

Dragonflies can fly both forward and backward! They rest with their wings held open.

Meadowhawk Dragonfly

E is for Earwig

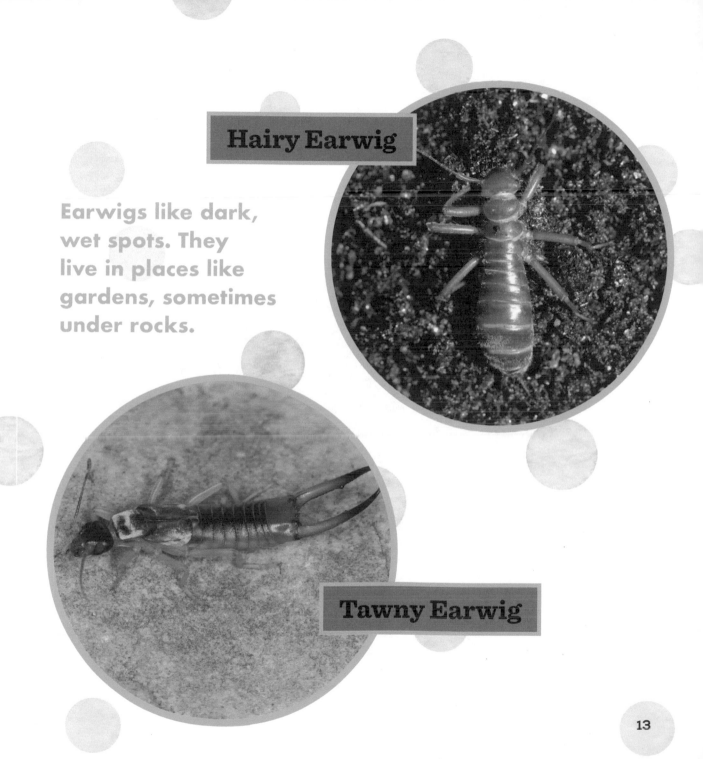

Hairy Earwig

Earwigs like dark, wet spots. They live in places like gardens, sometimes under rocks.

Tawny Earwig

F is for **Firefly**

Common Eastern Firefly

Fireflies are beetles that can light up in the dark. Some blink lights to "talk" together.

Glowworm

15

G is for **Grasshopper**

Rainbow Grasshopper

Grasshoppers are active during the day. They make sounds by rubbing their legs against their wings.

Eastern Lubber Grasshopper

H is for Honey Bee

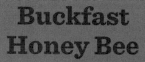
Buckfast Honey Bee

Some insects talk to each other with smells. When honey bees send out a danger warning, it smells like bananas!

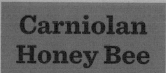
Carniolan Honey Bee

I is for **Ichneumon Wasp**

Giant Ichneumon Wasp

Ichneumon (*ick-NOO-muhn*) wasps are big. Giant ichneumon wasps have a body almost 2 inches long!

Yellow and Black Ichneumon Wasp

J is for Jewel Bug

Red Jewel Bug

Jewel bugs are colorful bugs that use their mouths to suck juice from plants.

Metallic Shield Bug

K is for Katydid

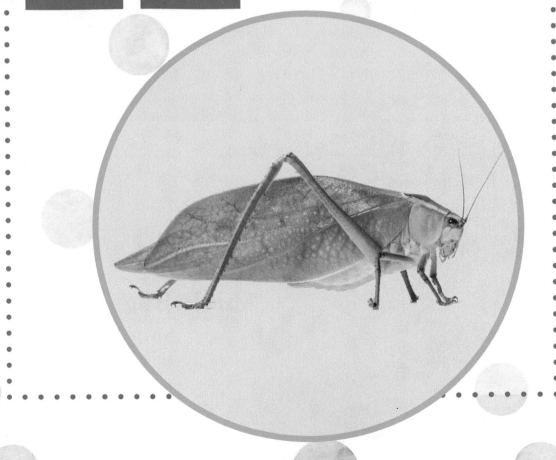

Lichen Katydid

Katydids "sing" by rubbing their wings together. Their chirps sound like they're saying, "Katy-did, Katy-didn't."

Spiny Devil Katydid

L is for **Ladybug**

Pine Ladybird

A ladybug is actually a beetle! Some have spots on their backs that help keep predators away.

Fourteen-Spotted Lady Beetle

M is for Moth

Moths may look like butterflies, but they have different types of antennae. Most fly at night.

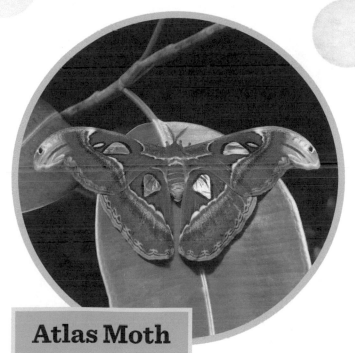

Atlas Moth

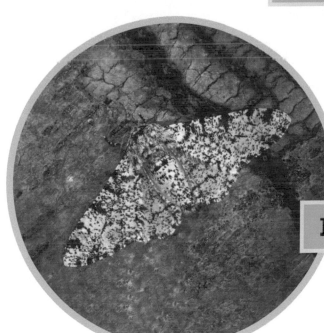

Peppered Moth

N is for Net-Winged Beetle

Banded Net-Winged Beetle

This beetle's colors warn predators that it tastes terrible!

End-Band Net-Winged Beetle

O

is for **Owlfly**

Split-eyed Owlfly

An owlfly is a fast-flying insect with a dragonfly-like body and a butterfly-like head. They have large owl-like eyes.

Owly Sulphur

P is for Praying Mantis

Orchid Mantis

A praying mantis's two front legs are spiky and folded. They use their legs to catch prey.

Giant Dead Leaf Mantis

Q is for Queen Bee

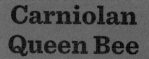

Carniolan Queen Bee

A queen bee is the largest bee in a colony. The colony needs the queen to survive.

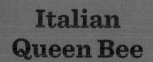

Italian Queen Bee

R is for **Rhinoceros Beetle**

Three-Horned Rhinoceros Beetle

Rhinoceros beetles are large and strong! Some rhinoceros beetles battle against each other.

Hercules Beetle

S is for Stick Insect

Giant Walking Stick

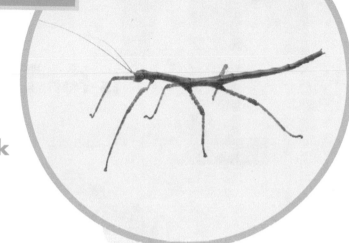

Stick insects have long bodies and skinny legs that look like sticks. They can blend in on trees and branches.

Thorny Stick Insect

T is for **Treehopper**

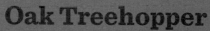

Treehoppers are small and live in trees. They shake their bodies to "talk" to each other.

Keeled Treehopper

U

**is for
Umbrella Wasp**

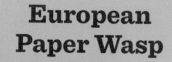

**European
Paper Wasp**

**Northern
Paper Wasp**

Umbrella wasps
chew wood to
make a paper nest.
Their nest looks like
an upside-down
umbrella.

V

is for Velvet Ant

Red Velvet Ant

Velvet ants aren't actually ants—they're wasps! They have velvety fur on their bodies.

Thistledown Velvet Ant

W is for Weevil

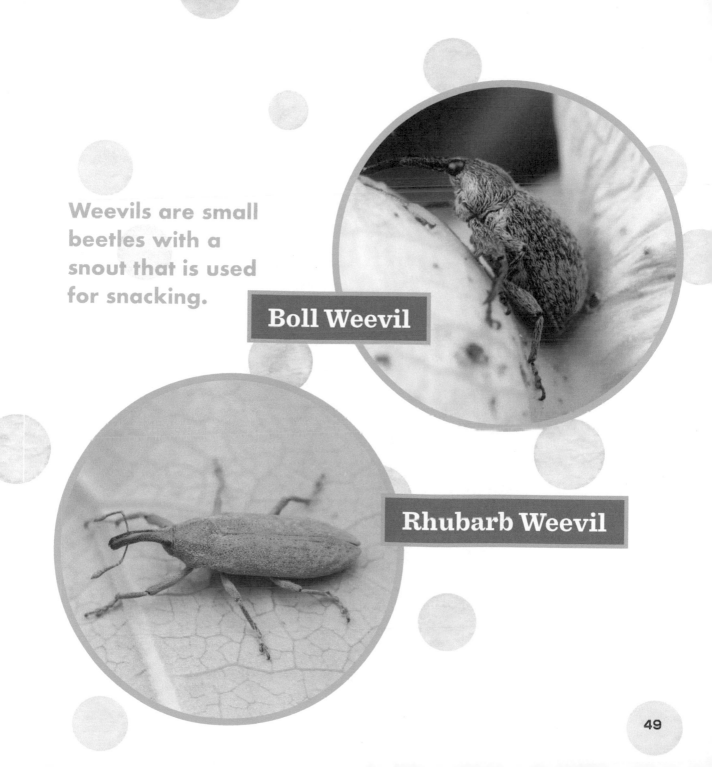

Weevils are small beetles with a snout that is used for snacking.

Boll Weevil

Rhubarb Weevil

49

X

**is for
Xystodesmidae**

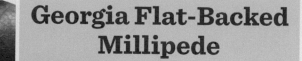

Georgia Flat-Backed Millipede

Xystodesmidae (*ziss-toe-DES-mih-dee*) is a family of millipedes, which are arthropods (*AHR-thruh-pods*), not insects.

Cyanide Millipede

51

Y is for Yellowjacket

Yellowjackets are a type of wasp that builds a large nest to live in together. They all have jobs to do.

Southern Yellowjacket

Bald-Faced Hornet

Z
is for
Zebra Spider

Zebra Spider

Zebra spiders have black and white stripes, and they jump to catch prey. Spiders are arthropods, not insects.

Zebra Spider jumping

About the Author

Jessica Lee Anderson is the author of over 50 books for children. When not writing, she enjoys planting a variety of flowers to welcome pollinators like bees and butterflies to her garden. Jessica also raises a variety of butterflies with her daughter, Ava, and husband, Michael. Visit JessicaLeeAnderson.com for more information.